RAIL TRANSIT PHILADELPHIA
THE PTC YEARS
1940-1968

MODERN, COURTEOUS SERVICE

RICHARD VIBLE AND HENRY ELSNER

N.J. International Inc.
1992

TABLE OF CONTENTS

(Front Cover) The Swann Memorial fountain at Logan Circle on the Benjamin Franklin Parkway provides a backdrop for the Peter Witt car typical of the city's transit in the Philadelphia Transportation Company (PTC) era. September 1955. (AS)

(Rear Cover) Work car W-54, a 1924 product of the local carbuilder J.G. Brill, at the Courtland Shops, July 1967. (AS)

Published by N.J. International, Inc. 77 West Nicholai St., Hicksville, N.Y. 11801

LC No. 92-080802

ISBN 0-934088-28-4

Copyright 1992

Printed in Hong Kong

No. 7613

PREFACE

Response to *Rail Transit Philadelphia - 20 Colorful Years, 1969-1989* has prompted the compilers of that volume to look back at the immediately preceding decades of street railway transportation in the Quaker City. The time threshold for stable dyes in amateur color photgraphy appears to be about 1939; we have therefore begun this survey at approximately that point. As might be expected, however, the bulk of available material dates to a later period, well within "The PTC Years" (1940-1968). Those 29 years saw the Philadelphia Transportation Company (PTC) replace the former Philadelphia Rapid Transit Company (PRT), in turn yielding control to the current operator, Southeastern Pennsylvania Transportation Authority (SEPTA).

The focus of this book is necessarily different from that of *20 Colorful Years*. Instead of calling attention to varied paint schemes (although the careful reader will spot a perhaps surprising number) sections are organized around the different streetcar types in use at the time, from the fabled Nearsides through the diminutive Birneys to the growing fleet of PCC streamliners. A secondary focus is on randomly selected but reasonably representative scenes on a number of routes in urban and countryside settings. Most, like the cars that served them, are long gone.

The photographs present a picture not only of a largely vanished mode of transportation, but of an urban setting which is also now only a part of history. The bustling industrial activity implied in many of the views has increasingly become stilled as economic functions and locations have changed. Residential dispersion has also had its effect. The distinctive Philadelphia rowhouse architecture remains today, but some neighborhoods have all but disappeared, along with their vibrant small-scale commercial strips. It is not only the motorman winding up his K-controller and banging on his foot gong who has vanished forever.

Readers will note that several topics included in *20 Colorful Years* have been omitted here. We did not feel it possible in one book on this time period to cover both the city and suburban systems. The Red Arrow trolleys and the Philadelphia & Western have therefore not been included. Since the Broad Street Subway equipment was shown in the earlier book, it was not repeated. However, although always an independent operation, never a part of PTC or predecessor PRT, the Fairmount Park Transit is such a fondly remembered part of Philadelphia's past that it had to be included.

This survey is not intended as a history or equipment roster. The several works by Harold E. Cox provide comprehensive treatment of those topics. Technical and historical data used here have been adapted from his *Surface Cars of Philadelphia, 1911-1965* (1965); *Utility Cars of Philadelphia, 1892-1971(1971); The Road from Upper Darby* (1967); and *The Fairmount Park Trolley, A Unique Philadelphia Experiment* (1970). Recommended for a brief but thorough introduction (as of 1954) is *Rail Transit in Philadelphia* by Joseph M. Mannix, published by the Philadelphia Chapter of the National Railway Historical Society, now out of print.

Credit for this volume really belongs to the dedicated photographers who have kindly made their work available (credits as indicated in parentheses): Anthony Sassa, including part of the Ray Muller collection (AS), David H. Cope (DC), Joseph M. Mannix (JM), and Theodore M. Meyers (TM). Our thanks to all of them for their generosity and patience. Frustrating attempts to obtain quality reproduction of decades-old originals were finally made successful through the skilled work of Edward Sharretts. His contribution has indeed been crucial. Finally, our gratitude is extended to all those in the Philadelphia transit-hobbyist fraternity who have shared their knowledge of time, place, and technical esoterica.

Henry Elsner, Jr.
Richard Vible
Philadelphia, Pa.
April 1, 1992

NEARSIDES

On any number of grounds, Philadelphia's Nearside cars can be awarded the title of most distinctive type ever to operate in the city. Built by hometown carbuilder J.G. Brill from 1911 to 1913, at 1500 strong they dominated the Philadelphia transit scene until 1948 and may have been the largest group of standardized cars delivered anywhere in the world. The name (properly Near Side but popularly combined into one word) is from the patented design emphasizing the safety and efficiency of boarding and unloading passengers at the vehicle's front door while paused at the "near side" instead of the "far side" of an intersection. Far-side loading had been the nearly universal practice employed on the rear-entrance cars typical of the era. The Nearside cars were also a pioneering large-scale instance of the arch-roof design, in contrast to the traditional deck or clerestory roof, and were an early attempt at a production model high-capacity, relatively lightweight car.

As originally built, not only for Philadelphia but in smaller numbers for Buffalo, Chicago, Atlantic City, and Lincoln, Nebraska, the cars had double front doors for both entrance and exit, with only a single emergency exit on the small rear platform; the conductor's position was at the front of the car. This arrangement was slow in loading and unloading, and hardly encouraged passengers to "step to the rear" when faced with the prospect of moving all the way forward again to exit. As a consequence, between 1919 and 1921, 1160 of the cars were fitted with double center-exit doors. The former single rear emergency exit was replaced with a body panel. Experiments with the conductor's position finally located it on the right side of the car immediately forward of the center doors. This duplicated the Peter Witt arrangement (named after the Cleveland transit commissioner who had invented it) and royalties were paid to its patent holders.

The resulting fleet was unique to Philadelphia, as the Nearside cars in the other cities retained the original door configuration. Most of the unaltered Philadelphia cars were converted to one-man operation in the 1920s, but the door

About a year before the PTC takeover of Philadelphia Rapid Transit, car 7002, newly delivered from the paint shop, at Frankford carbarn. It was the practice to let freshly-painted cars sit outside to dry thoroughly, with windows open to aid the process, before being returned to service. (JM)

problem remained, and the last of them was withdrawn in 1936. Meanwhile, beginning in 1933, many of the center-door Nearsides were equipped for one-man service. As such, they were "the workhorses of the system" (Cox) in the Depression years, finally being displaced by equipment shifts following large-scale arrival of PCC cars in 1941-42.

One of the last lines to use Nearsides, in 1955, was route 15, pictured here. Final Nearside operation was on route 64 in September, 1955. All but one of the cars were scrapped. The survivor, 6618, which had been equipped for instruction purposes, was donated to the Seashore Trolley Museum in Maine, where it remains today.

At Cumberland and Salmon on route 39, passing typical Philadelphia rowhouses. June 1949. (AS)

Northbound 6170 on route 23 is about to pass under the Pennsylvania Railroad's Whitemarsh Branch bridge at Cresheim Valley Drive. At the time of the photo, electric trains of MP-54 commuter cars rolled overhead. Today the right of way services only the Philadelphia Electric Company, but PCC cars still pass under the bridge at this scenic location. (DC)

Only a bit to the north of the previous scene, Mermaid loop still looks much the same, as PCC cars lay over in the spot held down by Nearside 6723. The slash through the route number indicates a short-turn run, a vehicle operating to a destination other than the end of the line. (DC)

5

The bucolic location at the edge of Fairmount Park is in sharp contrast to the somewhat grim setting of much of route 15. On Girard Avenue west of 33rd, just before crossing the bridge spanning the Schuykill River. (AS)

At Richmond and Allegheny, near the northeast end of route 15. PCC cars still serve this line and pass this intersection, but the tracks turning off to the left on Allegheny Avenue have been abandoned. June, 1949. (AS)

6

Car 6760 southbound on route 33 at 22nd and Allegheny, May 1953. The switches and curves were service track to and from the carbarn. (AS)

At the intersection of Norris and Richmond, in front of one of the buildings which once made Philadelphia " Workshop to the World." Westbound 6387 is turning into Norris. June 1949. (AS)

On Girard Avenue, east of Front Street, June 1949. (AS)

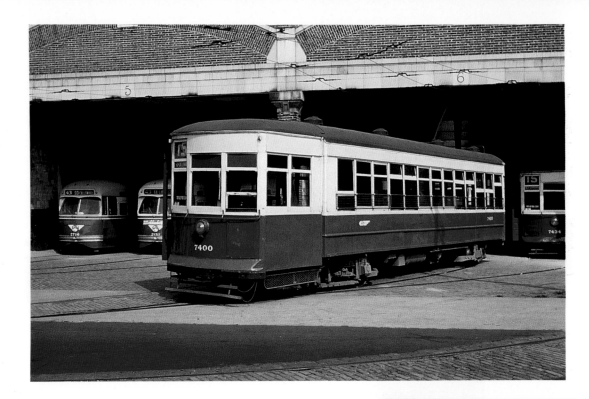

Callowhill barn, where Nearside 7400 once sat in the sun, is still in use, housing PCC cars of route 15 and Kawasaki LRVs for route 10. (TM)

"Upside Down" Nearside 7343 on 32nd at Ridge Avenue, with the Ridge barn complex at the rear. The sash sections were reversed on some Nearside cars to make window-cleaning easier—the safety guards were now unnecessary and did not have to be removed and reinstalled at each cleaning. (JM)

Right: "Paintliner" 6811 at Lehigh and Hancock, site of the PTC paint shop. Originally used as the designation for a class of rebuilt cars, the Paintliner label came to be applied to all cars given the color scheme shown on these two pages. May 1955. (AS) *Bottom, left:* Paintliner 7147 on route 9, Arch Street at 18th, ca. 1954. (RV) *Below, right:* The same car at 20th and Arch, westbound. The small rear platforms on the Nearside cars of necessity had drop sash instead of the distinctive "semi-convertible" type found in the car body. When fully raised, the semi-convertible sash slid completely into the car's roof, leaving a large breezy opening – a decided advantage in Philadelphia's humid summers. (RV)

HOGS

All 240 of the heavy, steel 4-motor double-end units delivered from Brill in 1918 became known as "Hog Island" cars or simply "Hogs" after the location of the World War I shipyard which many of them were built to serve. The title properly belongs only to the 100 cars in the 4000 series, equipped for multiple-unit operation. Trains of up to three cars carried workers from the 40th and Market elevated station to the shipyard, southwest of the city. With longitudinal bench seating, the cars were designed for capacity rather than passenger comfort. All but the final 30 were built for wartime federal agencies which later sold them to PRT.

Depression conditions saw many of the cars stored, with others converted to utility service; the 4000s remaining in use had the couplers removed. World War II again meant a demand for high-capacity equipment; stored units and those which had been converted to salt cars were rehabilitated for passenger service. Twenty of the MU cars had couplers replaced on one end to provide 2-car trains, designated as route 79S, running from the Philadelphia Quartermaster Depot at 20th and Johnston in South Philadelphia to the Navy Yard. With another change in ridership patterns after the war's end, the heavy, power-hungry cars again began to fade from the scene.

Throughout the entire period the Hogs had been a persistent presence on route 37, the interurban-like Chester Short Line (to the city of that name) and on heavy crosstown route 60, as reflected in some of the photos presented here.

The last 4000s were retired in 1955, the 5000s in 1956. Three 5000s then became work cars. Two of them were scrapped in the 1960s, while the third was destroyed in the Woodland carbarn fire of October 23, 1975. Three of the 4000s had been sold to the suburban Red Arrow Lines in 1942; one, number 26, is now in museum operation on Philadelphia's waterfront Penn's Landing Trolley. It is the only surviving Hog Island car.

In front of the Allegheny barn, Allegheny at 27th Street. The orange paint scheme indicated a rear-entrance car. (DC)

Allegheny at Ridge Avenue, the western stub-end of route 60. "Rear Entrance" sign denoted a 2-man car. (JM)

Left: In South Philadelphia, Snyder Avenue at 29th. (DC) *Below left:* Westbound on Allegheny at H Street, June 1949. (AS) *Below right:* Richmond carbarn, Allegheny and Richmond, was used as the eastern terminus of route 60 when double-end cars served the line. Cars ran to the back of the barn to reverse ends, then pulled to its front to lay over and load for the return trip. The Nearside car in the background, on route 15, is at the location shown on p.6, lower left. June 1949. (AS)

On Island Road in the Eastwick section of Philadelphia, a Chester Short Line car is southbound. Track on Island Road was laid in the gutter on each side of the roadway. (DC)

A change in the Hog's paint scheme and track work in progress indicate a later date than the preceding scene. The relocation of track to the median of a rebuilt Island Road made the former inbound track the new outbound route. (DC)

A short-turn loop, just inside the city, was located in the middle of open fields but designated 94th-Eastwick. The "Pay Leave" sign indicates an inbound subway-surface car: with heavy crowds going to Center City, most fares were paid in the subway upon exiting the station. Outbound trips were normal "Pay Enter," again due to subway loading, where most fares were collected by cashiers before the cars were boarded. (DC)

Inbound, below 94th Street. Newly installed battery-operated marker lights were for added safety in case of a dewirement in the subway. (DC)

On Industrial Highway beside the Baldwin Locomotive plant, approaching Eddystone. (DC)

Continuing south, the route crossed the Industrial Highway and would shortly approach Darby Creek. (DC)

An unusual A-frame bridge with gauntlet track in a wooden-planked roadway passed over Darby Creek, one of several streams crossed along the route. (DC)

Crossing Ridley Creek, entering the city of Chester. (DC)

At Wanamaker Avenue, Essington. Cars are being turned back here because of a spectacular trolley-truck collision and fire on the Crum Creek bridge, August 28, 1946 which ended through rail service to Chester. On November 24 the line was cut back from Wanamaker Avenue to a new loop at the Westinghouse plant in Lester. (DC)

5200s

As part of a massive modernization program launched in 1923, PRT purchased 135 new double-end cars from Brill. Similar in appearance to the Hogs, the two-motor cars (numbered consecutively from 5200) were mounted on the builder's familiar 39E2 maximum-traction trucks and so were lighter and more economical to operate. The wooden seating favored by management for sanitary reasons was arranged in two staggered sets of cross seats facing a longitudinal bench.

Over the years the cars saw repeated modification for one/two and one-man operation as well as alterations to front, rear, and offside door controls. A final rebuilding begun in 1941 supplied 16 cars with quiet herringbone gearing, improved brakes, lowered front destination signs, new flooring, and leather-upholstered seats. Because of the war, no further cars were done, although some did receive the new gears.

Postwar abandonments reduced the double-end fleet. The final runs of 5200s took place on August 11, 1957 when West Philadelphia route 46, pictured here, was abandoned. All but three of the cars were scrapped in 1955-57. Car 5326 is in operation at the Arden Trolley Museum near Pittsburgh. The other two are in the Philadelphia area, awaiting restoration.

A route 81 car takes the crossover before changing ends and reversing direction at the west end of the line, 31st and Passyunk Avenue, October 1955. (AS)

On Bridge Street at Frankford Avenue. (JM).

At 18th and Snyder, South Philadelphia. The bus is a training vehicle for the replacement service. October 1956. (AS)

Once again at the western end of route 60 in North Philadelphia, Allegeny and Ridge Avenues, May 1956. (AS)

At 6th Street, a route 60 car turns onto Erie Avenue on its pull-in trip to Luzerne barn. (AS)

20

Westbound on Passyunk at 28th Street at a time when modernity rather than energy efficiency was being plugged by "Reddy Kilowatt." October 1955. (AS)

The rowhouses on 58th Street and Greenway are typical of those still found in many West Philadelphia neighbor-hoods. Car 5223 is southbound, ca. 1956. (AS)

On 60th between Girard Avenue and Thompson, ca. 1956. (AS)

A route 46 car on 58th Street crosses the PRR's Media branch. (DC)

End of the line: 58th and Woodland Avenue loop. (DC)

On Chelten Avenue at Sydenham Street, in the northern section of the city. Row housing still, but of a somewhat more elegant style. (JM)

Route 66, in Northeast Philadelphia, was (and is) one of the heaviest surface routes, despite the rural appearance of these locations near and at the City Line terminus. The area is completely built up today; route 66 is now a trolleybus operation. August 1949 (AS)

Modernized 5327 on Chelten Avenue at Ogontz and Stenton Avenues. (JM)

Only the modernized cars carried PCC-style headlight wings. On Chelten Avenue at Greene Street. (AS)

On route 59, the Bustleton Surface Line, cutting through Oxford Circle, southbound. April 1949. (AS)

The outer portion of the Bustleton line was a single-track, country trolley route. Bustleton Avenue at Pennypack Park. (DC)

The north end of route 59 was in this pleasant setting, Bustleton and Lott Street. Part of route 59 is still served by trolleybuses. (DC)

8000s

The dominant cars throughout most of the PTC years were the 535 8000-series (known locally as "eighty hundreds"), Brill-built from 1923 to 1926, riding on 39E2 trucks. Operated as two-man, one-man or one/two-man cars, some for a time had such exotic arrangements as a center-door turnstile, or sealed center doors, the latter a revival of the old Nearside concept. During 1940-41, 373 of the cars were modernized in the same fashion as the smaller group of 5200s.

The 8000s were operating on 19 routes at the end of 1954, but began disappearing rapidly as conversions of rail routes accelerated after 1955. The last ones, running on Market Street, Philadelphia's main east-west artery, were withdrawn in December, 1957. Three cars were preserved, but none are currently in public operation.

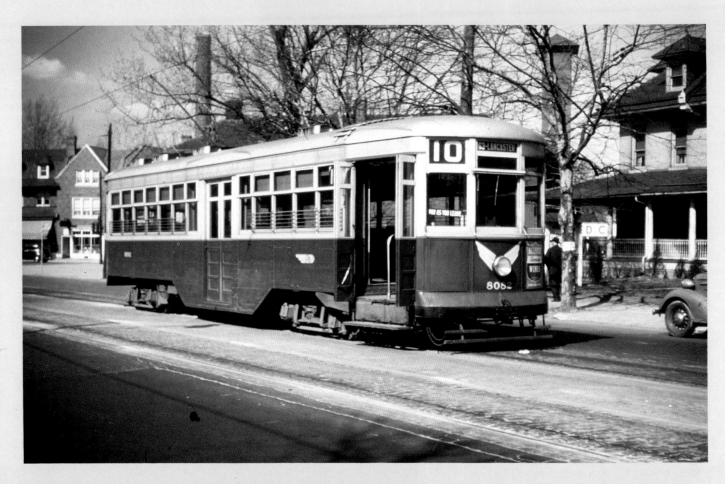

Rather flamboyant headlight wings and a silver letterboard with red trim distinguish modernized 8082. This was the style originally dubbed Paintliner. The car is on route 10's former loop track on 63rd Street between Lancaster Avenue and Malvern, West Philadelphia. (JM)

Above: Looking east from the front of the PRR (now Amtrak) 30th Street Station at a time when the trolley and rapid transit subway ended on the east side of the Schuylkill River. The area occupied by the elevated structure and streetcar tracks is today used for roadways and parking. New lighting now dramatically highlights the station building just out of sight to the left in this view. (DC) *Above right:* Across the river from the previous scene, looking west, with 30th Street Station in the right background. (JM) *Right:* A route 50 pull-out at 10th and Luzerne, opposite Luzerne barn. This track is still active. March, 1950. (AS)

A gritty urban setting, South Street at 13th in Center City Philadelphia. After a period of decline, South Street has experienced a revival, but at a cost, many would feel, of its authenticity. (JM)

On the old Gray's Ferry bridge over the Schuylkill River, a route 12 car inbound from West Philadelphia, August 1955. (AS)

Car 8143 turns from Woodland Avenue onto Island Road, West Philadelphia. All the track here is still in use; the red brick paving succumbed to a track relay project within the last few years. August 1955. (AS)

On Island Road, within sight of the previous location (past the PRR bridge at the upper left). Tracks leading to the right enter Elmwood Loop; the area on the hill above them is the site of the new Elmwood carbarn. August 1955. (AS)

The Parkside loop, opposite Fairmount Park, in West Philadelphia. Only buses turn here today. (AS)

29

In the precincts of the University of Pennsylvania, car 8022 bound for Center City on Spruce Street near 34th. The University Hospital at left, Houston Hall at right, still look the same. Tracks are gone from this section of Spruce Street, but the University is served by two underground subway-surface stops at 36th and 37th Streets. August 1956. (AS)

Route 62 was a one-car shuttle between Darby and Yeadon loops. The track is now operated as part of route 13 peak-hour trips. Visible in this scene are scars from former Birney route 78, which crossed and turned at this point. Tenth and Summit, Darby, August 1956. (AS)

30

Car 8335 turns at 33rd and York, September 1955. (AS)

Again, the industrial city: factories and warehouse, railroad tracks, working-class row homes. Nineteenth and Washington in South Philadelphia, crossing PRR tracks, June 1957. (AS)

At 18th Street in Center City, 8125 is eastbound on Market Street. Both the Stanley and Mastbaum are gone — and so is the unbelievably low-rise skyline.

Philadelphia's City Hall is in the middle of the Broad/Market Streets intersection. Streetcars, as all traffic today, had to circle the structure, out of sight at the right. The ornate building in the background, on North Broad Street, is the Masonic Temple. October 1957. (AS)

On the waterfront: route 32 cars entering, and about to leave, the loop at Front and Market Streets. June 1957. (AS)

Football games at Municipal Stadium in South Philadelphia were the occasion for a lineup of extra cars. At a Navy/Notre Dame game in the fall of 1957, Peter Witt cars are already outnumbered by PCCs. On 11th Street at Terminal Avenue, October 1957. (AS)

Car 8000 on a short piece of right of way shared by routes 9 and 48 on the Benjamin Franklin Parkway at 23rd Street. October 1955. (AS)

At 19th and Arch Streets, Center City. September 1955. (AS)

On 18th at Snyder Avenue. The home-delivery coal truck has disappeared along with the trolley car. (AS)

On 2nd at Lehigh in North Philadelphia car 8479 is southbound despite a northbound destination sign. On route 57, May 1955. (AS)

Route 26 had a stretch of roadside running on Oxford Avenue in the Burholme section of Philadelphia. Location is just south of a crossing with the Reading Railroad's Newtown branch. (AS)

Southbound on Oxford Avenue at the Reading crossing. Route 50 ran to Fox Chase only in peak hours. (JM)

BIRNEYS

Perhaps predictably, conservative Philadelphia never succumbed to the transit industry's craze for the small, single-truck "Safety Car" developed by Charles O. Birney which swept much of the country in the World War I period. Only 40 of the cars saw service on the Philadelphia area system. Ten of them had been purchased second-hand, while five were owned not by PRT or PTC but by the City of Philadelphia.

Most of the little cars were used on a network of lightly traveled single-track cross-country lines in Delaware County, southwest of Philadelphia. Known as the Folsom division, after the carbarn location, the three main routes connected Darby, Chester, and Media; two additional lines were also operated. Service on the Folsom division ended in 1939. Those cars still serviceable from the 25 bought in 1919 were all scrapped. The ten second-hand cars were presumably then used on Philadelphia shuttle services; the last four were scrapped in 1947.

Longest-lived of the cars were the five bought by the city in 1922, near the end of the Birney production era, and appropriately numbered 1-5. They were purchased for the new Bustleton Surface Line, route 59, built by the city as a connection from the Frankford elevated to a then undeveloped section of Northeast Philadelphia. The cars soon proved inadequate and were transferred to West Philadelphia shuttles in exchange for 5200s assigned to route 59. Despite an eventual repainting with PTC emblems, the cars remained city-owned until their final service, in 1948, on route 14.

Car 1027, at the Folsom barn, 1939, was one purchased from the Pennsylvania-New Jersey Railway, Trenton. The second-hand cars had four instead of three roof ventilators, and lacked the small window in the right front corner post. (JM)

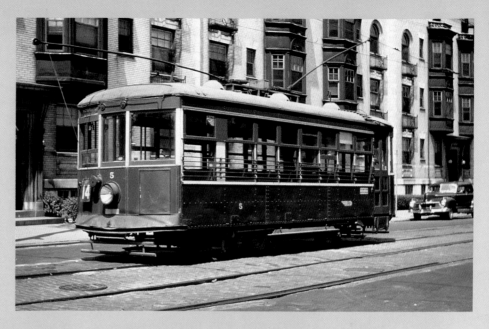

West Philadelphia shuttle route 14 had one terminus at 42nd and Chester. Car 5 of the city-owned group pauses before taking the crossover to begin its run back to 40th and Market Streets. An inbound Peter Witt car crosses Baltimore Avenue in the background. The 42nd Street track today continues across Chester Avenue as part of the subway-surface diversion route. (DC)

Another view of car 5, seen from the sidewalk on the right hand side of the previous scene. This section of 42nd Street still looks much the same. (DC)

At the Darby loop, just west of Philadelphia, terminal for several lines including shuttle 78. Route 78 is long gone, but the loop, including this trackage, is now served by the Kawasaki cars of route 13. (DC)

Car 4 at the other end of route 78, Wycombe at Fairview in Lansdowne. The operator has changed ends and is about to depart for Darby. (DC)

PCC AIR CARS

In 1938, only two years after the first production models of the fast, quiet, and streamlined PCC (Presidents' Conference Committee) cars were introduced nationally, 20 appeared on Philadelphia streets. Ordered for route 53, the new cars were presented in a striking livery of silver with blue trim. Under the new PTC management, 130 more were delivered in 1940-41, with 110 following in 1942. Separate number series were used for cars initially equipped for one- or two-man operation. All, generally similar in external appearance, were referred to as "prewar" or "air cars," the latter term a reference to the use of conventional air compressors to provide force for part of the braking cycle and to power auxiliary equipment for door and other mechanisms. In a departure from the Brill tradition, the cars were built by the St. Louis Car Company.

The 20 cars dating from 1938 were scrapped in 1960. The rest of the air-car fleet lasted through the PTC era, but was gradually reduced in subsequent years as rail operation contracted. The last cars were withdrawn in January, 1983. Three cars have survived, but none are currently operational.

Car 2004 from Philadelphia's first PCC order, northbound on route 53, Erie Avenue at Germantown. The wedge-shaped grille on the trolley shroud was unique to this car. (DC)

On the route 53 loop at 10th and Luzerne, car 2015 from the original PCC group has had its silver livery replaced by the gray roof variant of PTC's standard green and cream. March 1950. (AS)

Cars of the next PCC order were also originally painted silver. At the 61st and Pine Street end of West Philadelphia's route 42. (JM)

On The Warpath in Philadelphia

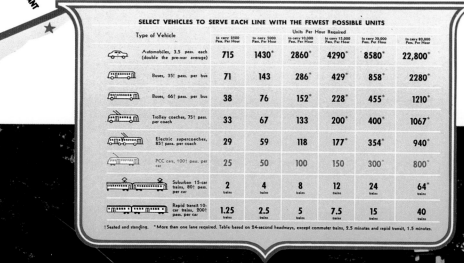

WAR PLANT WAR PLANT WAR PLANT WAR PLANT WAR PLANT WAR PLANT WAR PLANT WAR PLANT

57 VICTORY VEHICLES ARE CARRYING

2,000,000 Passengers per Month

SELECT VEHICLES TO SERVE EACH LINE WITH THE FEWEST POSSIBLE UNITS

Type of Vehicle		to carry 2500 Pass. Per Hour	to carry 5000 Pass. Per Hour	to carry 10,000 Pass. Per Hour	to carry 15,000 Pass. Per Hour	to carry 30,000 Pass. Per Hour	to carry 80,000 Pass. Per Hour
				Units Per Hour Required			
	Automobiles, 3.5 pass. each (double the pre-war average)	715	1430*	2860*	4290*	8580*	22,800*
	Buses, 35† pass. per bus	71	143	286*	429*	858*	2280*
	Buses, 66† pass. per bus	38	76	152*	228*	455*	1210*
	Trolley coaches, 75† pass. per coach	33	67	133	200*	400*	1067*
	Electric supercoaches, 85† pass. per coach	29	59	118	177*	354*	940*
	PCC cars, 100† pass. per car	25	50	100	150	300*	800*
	Suburban 15-car trains, 80† pass. per car	2 trains	4 trains	8 trains	12 trains	24 trains	64 trains
	Rapid transit 10-car trains, 200† pass. per car	1.25 trains	2.5 trains	5 trains	7.5 trains	15 trains	40 trains

† Seated and standing. * More than one lane required. Table based on 24-second headways, except commuter trains, 2.5 minutes and rapid transit, 1.5 minutes.

THE Philadelphia Transportation Company's 263 PCC cars are helping to carry traffic that has rocketed 32 per cent above the January, 1941, record. But on Route 56, the heavy war industries have shoved the transit load up 56 per cent—far above the city's average.

How does PTC carry the war workers on Route 56? With PCC cars, of course. These big, modern street cars, with the greatest passengers-per-hour capacity of any surface vehicle, are the logical choice for transit's biggest jobs. Consuming no gas, using no rubber tires, they conserve these vital materials.

More Cars—700,000 More Passengers per Month!

Yes, believe it or not, they've added only 13 more cars on this route since January, 1941—and absorbed an increase of 700,000 passengers per month. How is it possible? By carrying as many as 100 passengers per car, on peak-hour headways of 1 to 1½ minutes.

Each Platform Man Averages 990 Riders per Day

Man power is scarce but PTC tries to keep man power worries at the minimum. On Route 56 an average of 990 passengers per platform man carried on weekdays illustrates how their big carrying capacity, make the most efficient use of man power.

The street car requires fewer maintenance men, too, because it has fewer wearing parts than other vehicles.

Electric Transit—Your Best Bet in War and Peace

Remember the outstanding job these cars are doing when you can again obtain transit vehicles. In war or in peace, your heavily traveled lines will thrive on the advantages of modern electric transit. Streamlined, economical, swift, and clean—these are the features which attract riders. And because street cars have the *biggest passengers-per-hour capacity of any surface vehicle*, you can always be sure that they will be best able to carry the crowds—in comfort. *General Electric, Schenectady, N. Y.*

How to Get Parts a Year from Now

With materials scarce, and manufacturing capacity overtaxed, it is becoming increasingly difficult to meet the rush for renewal parts. To make sure that YOU have renewal parts when you need them, we suggest the following simple procedure. Estimate your renewal parts requirements for a year ahead (on the basis of previous requirements and anticipated mileage), decide when deliveries are desired, and forward this schedule to your G-E representative. Then your parts requirements can be scheduled along with the manufacture of other essential war materials.

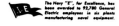

The Navy "E", for Excellence, has been awarded to 92,780 General Electric employees in six plants manufacturing naval equipment.

"They're Getting Workers to Production Lines on Time," says R. T. Senter

"In addition to supplying the normal transportation needs of the nation's third largest city—Philadelphia Transportation Company is supplying service for 400,000 war workers. To do this tremendous job, there is urgent need for all the capacity we can obtain. We have pressed into service every available vehicle using each type—buses, trolley coaches, and street cars—in the kind of service to which it is best suited. One of our most important war routes is Route 56, served by PCC cars. This route cuts across the north and northeast section of the city and covers an area honeycombed with important war-production centers. The PCC cars are doing a splendid job getting workers to production lines safely, dependably, and on time. We are placing the last of 110 more PCC cars in service."

GENERAL ⒼⒺ ELECTRIC

107-92-9663

R. T. Senter
President
Philadelphia Transportation Company

The view west from the front of the B&O station, with the Main Post Office building across the river, August 1956. (AS)

Trolleys on Chestnut Street passed the Baltimore and Ohio Railroad station at 24th Street, just east of the Schuylkill River. The ornate structure, designed by Philadelphia architect Frank Furness, was destroyed by fire in the early 1960s. (JM)

One block to the north of the previous location, trolley and rapid transit tracks emerged from the Market Street subway to cross the Schuylkill River. An outbound car on route 37 is about to pick up a passenger at the 24th Street station. (DC)

A route 38 car in front of 30th Street Station, after leaving the subway and crossing the river. (The same location was shown on p.27.) The "Welcome to Philadelphia" sign is atop the Gimbels warehouse on Chestnut at 24th, across the street from the B&O station. September 1955. (AS)

THE dream of extending the Market Street Subway into West Philadelphia, permitting removal of the bridge over the Schuylkill and all of the Elevated structure east of 46th st., will become a reality this month.

It is a dream that has persisted for a number of years, during which time the plans were improved and the undertaking was expanded to include an extension of the surface-car subway to 40th st. & Woodland ave.

These twin highspeed transit improvements, projects of the City of Philadelphia in which PTC has collaborated, will furnish faster service for thousands of riders of the subway-surface lines and help speed traffic in the University of Pennsylvania-Drexel Institute of Technology-Pennsylvania Station area, where some of the worst bottlenecks in the city exist. They will also change the face of Market st. west of the Schuylkill River.

You will soon be riding in these new facilities. And if you are a subway-surface rider, you have the further advantage of riding in the modern, streamlined cars that have been running on the subway-surface lines since early in September.

Construction of the new subway tubes has been a difficult and intricate job. Because service had to be maintained throughout the construction period, the job was particularly complex in the vicinity of 22d & Market sts. where the new and old tubes join and where a new subway-surface station has been built.

Completion of the new subways was brought about under the direction of the City's Department of Public Property headed by Commissioner Mortin E. Rotman and the Department's Engineering Branch under Howard S. Hipwell.

The changeover to actual operation in the new tubes is similarly complex, and will be accomplished in three steps on three different weekends, beginning Friday night, October 14. Details of this changeover are shown in the box on page 6.

Three new subway stations

Extension of the Market Street Subway involved construction of three new subway stations, two of which are at new locations. The other is at 40th st., replacing the 40th St. Elevated Station.

The new locations are at 30th st. and 34th st., to better serve the changed face of West Philadelphia. They replace Elevated stations at 32d st. and 36th st. The Elevated station at 32d st. was, of course, placed there when the old West Philadelphia Station of the Pennsylvania Railroad stood at 32d st. — long before the beautiful station at 30th st. was even a planner's dream. The station at 36th st. evened up the distance between 32d and 40th sts.

The new 30th St. Subway Station will directly serve the railroad station, the Post Office and the new Bulletin buildings. Escalators provided by the Pennsylvania Railroad will bring passengers from the subway station (and also from the new subway-surface station at 30th st.) to the street-floor level of the railroad station.

Subway trains will emerge from the new tube just north of Market st. at 44th st., climb a ramp and swing back over Market st. to continue on the Elevated structure from the 46th St. Station westward.

SUBWAY TRAINS EMERGE AT 44TH ST

46th St. Elevated Station

40th St. Subway Station

MARKET ST. SUBWAY

34th St. Subway Station

30th St. Subway and Subway-Surface Stations

Bulletin Buildings

P.-R.-R. Station

RIVER

22d St. Subway-Surface Station

Route 10 EMERGES AT 36TH ST

33d St. Subway-Surface Station

U. S. Post Office

SCHUYLKILL

CHESTNUT

Sansom St. Subway-Surface Station

WALNUT

	SUBWAY
	ELEVATED
	SURFACE
	BUS ROUTE 38

Routes 11, 34 AND 37* EMERGE AT 40TH ST

37th St.-University Subway-Surface Station

Woodland Ave

BALTIMORE AVE

WOODLAND AVE

* Route 37 to be consolidated with Route 36, beginning Sunday, November 6. See page 5 of this folder.

PTC handout dated Oct. 13, 1955 details the Market-Frankford rapid transit and subway-surface changes that eliminated the trolley tracks and elevated structure shown on the proceding two pages. The changeover was completed on the weekend of Nov. 5-6.

47

PCC-equipped route 36, a remnant of the former Chester Short Line, passing through the wetland area just beyond the southwest edge of the city, as viewed from the Industrial Highway overpass. Route 36 still runs with Kawasaki cars, but has been cut back before this point. August 1956. (AS)

Further out on route 36, an inbound car leaves pavement for the rustic right of way, 5th Avenue and Powhattan Avenue, Lester. August 1956. (AS)

Route 36 terminal at the Westinghouse plant loop in Lester, August 1956. (AS)

Sixth and Main Streets, Darby. A route 11 car crosses the B&O main line. The energized wire mesh above the trolley wire was a patented safety device to insure that a car could not be stalled on the crossing by a trolley pole dewirement. The railroad's "tower" is gone, but Kawasaki cars still rumble across what is now a single track, the only remaining trolley-railroad grade crossing on the system. (AS)

A route 13 car at 5th and Chestnut in front of Independence Hall, out of sight on the left. September 8, 1956. (AS)

Parallel streets Chestnut and Walnut were one-way eastbound and westbound. Car 2609 on route 13 heads west at 6th and Walnut. A route 50 car is northbound in the background. (TM)

Service on Chestnut and Walnut was the last surface rail entry into Center City from the west. Its abandonment was the occasion for a vehicle parade on Monday, September 10, 1956. At 11th and Walnut. Regular operation had ceased the day before. (AS)

Crossing Market Street on 17th Street, south-bound, in Sunday service when line 21 was through-routed with 32 to South Philadelphia. In the background is the PRR Sububan Station building; the empty lot in the right foreground is the site of the former "Chinese Wall," the Pennsylvania Railroad's embankment leading to the Broad Street Station. (TM)

Car 2582, a gray-roof car without the customary maroon beltrail stripe, is in Sunday service at Paschall and 49th in West Philadelphia. (TM)

PCC 2070, at 54th and Woodland, was the only car to carry the standard bus livery, marked by a white roof and orange instead of maroon stripe. May 1958. (AS)

Seen from the elevated station at 52nd and Market, northbound 2606 is operating Sunday PCC service on route 70. (TM)

PCC 2648 turning from Old York Road onto Erie Avenue is a route 26 car going on-line via tracks of route 53. Route 26 was PCC-operated on weekends. (TM)

Looking west on Erie Avenue at "O" Street from the Erie-Torresdale elevated station. The streetcar is eastbound on route 56, a line still served by PCC cars. Track curving off to the left was a cutback loop for route 3. July 1958. (AS)

Through the car wash at Luzerne carbarn. February 1950. (AS)

PCC ALL-ELECTRICS

Philadelphia continued to add to its PCC roster in the early postwar period: 210 new cars arrived in 1947-48, again numbered in two series. The "all electric" vehicles dispensed with the air compressors of the earlier design, and were also quite different in appearance. Body windows were smaller and more numerous, with a second level of "standee" windows designed to allow standing passengers to look for street signs or landmarks without bending over seated patrons. The front windshield was also redesigned to reduce glare and reflection at the operator's position. Like the air cars, the all-electrics were St. Louis Car Co. products.

About 90 of the cars remain in Philadelphia in 1991, with the balance sold or scrapped.

Stalled in the snow: 2724 at 5th and Market, Feb. 8, 1967. A supervisor is coupling a drawbar to the following car for extra traction to break through the snow drift. (AS)

At Frankford Terminal, Frankford and Bridge Streets. (W.E. Robertson)

THE LATEST IN

Streamliners

Last week PTC welcomed the arrival of its first postwar shipment of streamlined street cars. The new cars feature all the up-to-the-minute safety and comfort devices. One of the latest improvements is the new "standee" window which permits a standing rider to see out on the street at a glance, without crouching to peer through the regulation window. Wider aisles make for easier boarding and exit, and the exit door has been moved farther to rear of the car.

At a cost of $2,131,000, a fleet of 100 of these fast, smooth-riding streamliners is being built for PTC. Most of them will be used to replace the conventional-type street cars now in service on Route 23, the Germantown ave. line. Route 23 is PTC's longest and most heavily traveled surface car line, carrying more than 100,000 passengers a day. It operates from 10th st. & Oregon ave. to Germantown ave. & Bethlehem Pike in Chestnut Hill, a distance of more than 12 miles.

In addition to these new cars, 110 more streamliners, 135 buses and 65 trackless trolleys are on order and scheduled for delivery this year.

The American PCC car seems out of place in a setting reminiscent of Europe as a route 47 northbound trip traverses the Italian Market on 9th Street in South Philadelphia, June, 1963. (RV)

On the long route 6 to Willow Grove, north of the city, an outbound car on Tyson Avenue crosses Susquehanna Road in Abington, June 1957. (AS)

Northbound on route 6 near Church Road in Cheltenham Township, February 1958. (AS)

Southbound in Cheltenham Township. The substation in the background has been converted to other uses, and the cut through which the car is running was filled for the construction of a high school after rail abandonment. February 1958. (AS)

Route 6 was noted for its scenic countryside right of way. At Royal Avenue, Glenside; r/w here was designated Keswick Avenue. February, 1958. (AS)

A once-character- istically American urban scene on "the Avenue": Ger- mantown at Erie, with a route 23 car northbound. The line and this type of car still serve this very heavy transfer point. (TM)

A route 60 car passing the former Richmond carbarn – a tire-retread plant at the time of the photo – turns from Richmond to Allegheny Avenue, June 1967. Car 2187 has been converted into a line car, with the same number. (RV)

On route 23, 11th and Montgomery Avenue. (TM)

MIDWESTERN MIGRANTS

As part of the postwar modernization program, 90 second-hand PCC cars were purchased in 1955, 50 from St. Louis and 40 from Kansas City. The St. Louis cars, a non-standard type, proved troublesome from the beginning of their Philadelphia service. The first ones were scrapped in 1956, and all were gone by 1962. The Kansas City all-electrics, unique in appearance because of the lack of standee windows, fared better. Most lasted well into the SEPTA years. A few have been sold or preserved, but none of them are now in use.

In their former owners' colors, ex St. Louis (foreground) and Kansas City (rear) cars at 2nd and Courtland, April 3, 1955. (AS)

A former St. Louis Public Service car, now PTC 2201, turns from Hunting Park Avenue to Erie Avenue at 22nd Street on route 56. (AS)

Kansas City 759 at 2nd and Courtland, April 3, 1955. (AS)

On route 5 at American and Oxford Streets, December 1955. (AS)

One of the former Kansas City cars on Broad Street and Government Avenue, near the Municipal Stadium, for the Navy/Notre Dame football game. October 1957. (AS)

A lineup of ex-Kansas City cars in the partially-demolished Frankford barn. December 1955. (AS)

61

BRILLINERS

Philadelphia's Brill company, once the world's largest street-car builder, failed to participate in producing the industry-designed PCC car. It chose to market a commercially unsuccessful competitor which it named the *Brilliner*. Superficially similar to the PCC, the Brilliner had a riveted rather than welded body, and rode on trucks designed by Brill. Three sample cars acquired by PTC in 1939 saw little service after World War II. Two were scrapped in 1951, the third in 1956.

On a chartered trip, the surviving Brilliner tours "Route Zero," the company training loop, at 2nd and Courtland. May, 1953. (AS)

On an earlier charter trip, car 2023 turns from Old York Road (route 55) to Chelten Avenue (route 52), ca. 1950. (AS)

WORK CARS

A large fleet of utility cars performed all the varied tasks essential to support a smoothly-functioning passenger service. Snow removal, overhead-wire and track maintenance, transportation of parts and supplies, all had their specialized vehicles. In the PTC years, many units dated from the same 1923 modernization program which produced the 5200s and 8000s; others were a miscellany of home-built vehicles or passenger-car conversions. Operating sporadically, often at night, they were among the most elusive of Philadelphia electric cars to photograph in service.

Car P-16 has just arrived at Luzerne barn with a load of overhauled motors from PTC's Kensington shops. A 1911 Brill product, P-16 lasted until 1956. (JM)

PTC owned a pier on the Delaware River for receipt of supplies by ship. Power for work cars there was provided by cable "snakes." Cars W-55 (Brill, 1924) and W-27 (home-built in 1908, scrapped 1952) in March, 1950. (AS)

W-29, company-built as an ash car in 1908, was rebuilt in 1913 and scrapped in 1955. The use to which the car was put is evident in this scene at southern barn, as are its distinctive Curtis trucks. (JM)

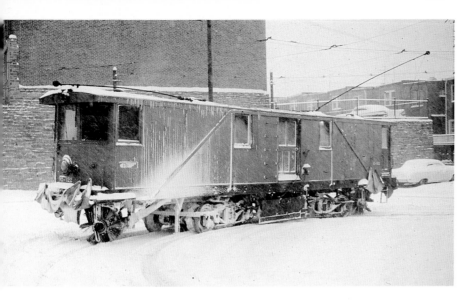

Large double-truck sweeper C-122 came from Brill in 1923. At 5th and Godfrey loop. (AS)

Sweeper C-39 in its element, 17th and Market westbound. (JM)

On Luzerne Street, east of 12th, beside Luzerne barn, February 1958. C-144, Brill-built as a plow in 1923, was converted to a sweeper in 1927. All trolley snow-fighting equipment was phased out in the SEPTA era. (AS)

Single-truck snow sweeper C-75, Frankford barn, was a home-built product of the 1890s. (JM)

About to be scrapped at Southern carbarn in April 1958, C-52 is another 1890s vintage home-made unit. (AS)

Sand car S-1 at Frankford barn. Two cars of this type were used to supply carbarn storage bins from which sand, needed to aid braking in difficult conditions, was replenished in individual cars' sand boxes. S-1, built by Brill in 1913, was scrapped in 1956. (JM)

U-34, ex 5001, was one of the Hogs which became a utility car. Photographed at Southern barn, 5001 survived until the Woodland carbarn fire of 1975. (JM)

Line car D-38, built by Brill in 1923, at Luzerne barn in September, 1951. (AS)

D-37 (Brill, 1922) at work dismantling route 37, October 1957. (AS)

SCRAPPING

Scrapping activity at Southern barn, April 1958, gives a closeup view of the Brill 39E type truck which propelled most of PTC's conventional cars. Peter Witt 8517 is next in line to be dismantled. (AS)

The dramatic scene at the Bailis scrapyard, 10th and Packer Avenue, was repeated in many places across the country as "The Time of the Trolley" ran out. January, 1958. (AS)

MARKET-FRANKFORD CARS

Throughout most of the PTC era the Market-Frankford subway-elevated line was served by but two types of equipment – appropriately enough named "Market Cars" and "Frankford Cars." Both sets were all-steel, closed-platform units of modest performance. The 215 Market cars, about 50 feet long and distinguished by the "railroad" clerestory roof, were delivered in eight lots between 1906 – in time for the line's March, 1907 opening – and 1913. All but the last 80 (Brill products) were built by Pressed Steel Car Co. of Pittsburgh. Overall appearance was similar to that of New York's IRT equipment of the period.

The longer (55 foot) arch-roofed Frankford cars, built by Brill in a single lot of 100 in 1922, were purchased by the City of Philadelphia for its Frankford Elevated Extension opening that November. Trains of both types then ran over the entire line, but individual cars were not intermixed.

Not until 1960 were any of the worn and aging cars replaced – and then all were retired at once as 270 new stainless-steel cars were delivered by the Budd Company. A few of the Frankford cars were retained for utility service, but are no longer in use.

A recently-shopped Market car glistens in the sun at 56th and Market, westbound. (JM)

Market cars head into the subway at 24th and Market, June 1949. (AS)

A train of the other type of equipment on the line, the Frankford cars, leaves the opposite end of the subway at Front Street and Market. This entrance to the subway has been realigned; the Benjamin Franklin Bridge in the background is the only other element in the scene remaining today. March, 1950. (AS)

Arrival of the first car in the Budd replacement fleet: City of Philadelphia 601 on Bridge Street near Penn, May 19, 1960. After 30 years of service on the Market-Frankford line, the car was re-equipped with standard-gauge trucks and placed in operation on the 69th Street to Norristown (P&W) route. (AS)

THE PARK TROLLEY

Whatever Philadelphians may have felt about the disappearance of their Nearsides and Peter Witts, there is unanimous agreement that the demise of Fairmount Park Transit – the "Park Trolley" – was a grevious loss. (Although as with much nostalgia, the affection is probably more real in memory than it was in practice. On the last holiday of operation, July 4, 1946 – after abandonment had been announced – 37,000 people were hauled; up to 100,000 a day had ridden in the early 1920s.) Built in 1897 to provide convenient access to the nation's largest city park, the 8-1/2 mile line was operated in two counter-clockwise loops: traffic was routed from each of the two terminals to the Woodside amusement park, at the northwest edge of the Fairmount Park. Service began with a fleet of 20 open motor cars and 30 open trailers, with 10 closed cars for winter service (operated as a single loop over the entire route). All of the cars were built by Brill.

The line ended operation on September 9, 1946 with the same cars – though somewhat diminished in number – rails, routes, and fixed facilities with which it began. Its Strawberry Mansion bridge across the Schuylkill River, complete with vacant double-track right of way beside the paved road, is still in use, as is the carbarn, now housing city utility vehicles. All other artifacts were removed, as stipulated at a post-abandonment auction, but much of the route can still be traced. None of the rolling stock was preserved.

Always physically and economically separate from the city's other transit services, the Park Trolley was never really profitable. But in this safety and environmentally-conscious age, perhaps a fitting final salute is this passage from the *Street Railway Journal* of August, 1897.

On reaching the park the visitor's first surprise is to find the cars standing in the edge of the lawn with almost nothing suggesting a railway in sight. While the usual overhead work is in place it is not conspicuous, owing to the openness of its surroundings, while on the ground only two rail heads are seen stretching away through the grass. The space between the rails is completely filled in and sown with grass. The element of danger is eliminated by avoiding, from one end of the park to the other, every grade crossing of even a foot path. The line dips sharply under many of the carriageways; it winds along valleys, clings to the hillsides, follows up and down ravines, and is as utterly unobtrusive as two lines of iron could be on the landscape.

This scene, at an unidentified stop in Fairmount Park, once was typical of summer service all across the country. The cross-bench open cars were crowded with town and city dwellers eager to sample the breezes produced by motion through a cooler countryside in the era before air-conditioning. The two-man crews included a roving conductor swinging along the running board to collect fares. Fairmount Park Transit, it should be noted, provided its motormen with a bit more comfort in inclement weather than most companies of the time by equipping the front platforms with window sash. September 7, 1946, two days before the end of regular service on the Park Trolley. (All photos this section, DC)

The rear platforms of the single-end cars remained open, an arrangement retained from time of construction, and typical of most cars of this type. September 7, 1946.

A motor-trailer set leaves Woodside Park, August 10. 1946.

Closed cars were used during the winter season and in cooler weather. The 5-cluster light at the station platform was traditional for the period, as the low-voltage bulbs, wired in series, could be fed directly from the propulsion current. April 4, 1946.

(Above) Car 10 again, and on the same day. Only two cars were required to operate the off-season schedule in the final years. The single-end cars had doors on both sides of the body. (Right) Through the woods on September 7, 1946.

The switchman's shanty at Greenland station. Track on the right leads to the bridge across the Schuylkill River and to the 33rd and Dauphin end of the line. Cars proceeding straight ahead serve the other terminal, at 44th and Parkside.

At the 33rd and Dauphin terminal, on the east side of the river. The closed cars also had open rear platforms. The controls there, including the goose-neck hand brake, were retained from the original double-end construction in order to aid movements into the carbarn. October 31, 1945.

Strawberry Mansion Bridge was built by the Park Trolley to provide service from across the Schuylkill River. Girders, railings, and trolley-wire supports reflect the style of the period. February 25, 1946.

The barn was deliberately built in a hollow, to be unobtrusive in the park setting. Building and cars are shabby one month after abandonment. October 6, 1946.

Right and facing page: In later years Fairmount Park Transit had one powered all-purpose work car, No. 200, rebuilt from closed passenger car 9. Photographed on September 7, 1946 at the barn, and later that year on one of the line's steel trestles during a pause in the car's final assignment, dismantling the Park Trolley.

Richard Vible, a native of Philadelphia with a longstanding interest in the history of the city and its transportation systems, is employed in the transit industry.

Henry Elsner, a transplanted midwesterner who has lived in Philadelphia since 1961, is associate editor of *Electric Lines.*